50 Instant Pot Soups and Stews for the Fall

By: Kelly Johnson

Table of Contents

- Pumpkin Soup
- Butternut Squash and Carrot Soup
- Classic Beef Stew
- Chicken Tortilla Soup
- Sweet Potato and Lentil Soup
- Spicy Pumpkin Chili
- Creamy Tomato Basil Soup
- Chicken and Wild Rice Soup
- Autumn Harvest Soup
- Butternut Squash Chili
- Italian Wedding Soup
- French Onion Soup
- Beef and Barley Stew
- Vegetable and Quinoa Soup
- Sausage and White Bean Stew
- Chicken and Corn Chowder
- Apple and Bacon Soup
- Potato Leek Soup
- Split Pea Soup with Ham
- Harvest Chicken Stew
- Sweet Potato and Black Bean Chili
- Cabbage Roll Soup
- Tuscan Bean and Kale Soup
- Mushroom and Barley Soup
- Beef and Sweet Potato Stew
- Curried Butternut Squash Soup
- Bacon and Potato Soup
- Carrot Ginger Soup
- Zucchini and Tomato Stew
- Spaghetti Squash and Sausage Soup
- Harvest Pumpkin Chili
- Corn and Potato Chowder
- Chicken Gnocchi Soup
- Tomato and Roasted Red Pepper Soup
- White Bean and Sausage Soup

- Lamb and Vegetable Stew
- Pork and Apple Stew
- Turkey and Sweet Potato Soup
- Beef and Mushroom Stew
- Creamy Broccoli Cheddar Soup
- Chicken and Dumplings
- Pork Posole
- Spicy Black Bean Soup
- Ham and Bean Soup
- Chicken and Kale Stew
- Wild Rice and Mushroom Soup
- Pumpkin and Sage Soup
- Shrimp and Corn Chowder
- Roasted Vegetable Soup
- Brussels Sprouts and Bacon Soup

Pumpkin Soup

Ingredients:

- 1 medium-sized pumpkin (about 4 cups of pumpkin flesh, peeled and cubed)
- 1 tablespoon olive oil
- 1 onion, chopped
- 2 garlic cloves, minced
- 1 carrot, peeled and chopped
- 1 potato, peeled and chopped
- 4 cups vegetable broth (or chicken broth)
- 1/2 teaspoon ground cumin
- 1/4 teaspoon ground cinnamon
- Salt and pepper, to taste
- 1/2 cup coconut milk or cream (optional, for a creamy texture)
- Fresh herbs (such as parsley or thyme) for garnish (optional)

Instructions:

1. **Prepare the pumpkin:** Peel, deseed, and cube the pumpkin. Set aside.
2. **Sauté the vegetables:** In a large pot, heat the olive oil over medium heat. Add the chopped onion and garlic, cooking until softened, about 5 minutes.
3. **Add the pumpkin and other veggies:** Stir in the cubed pumpkin, chopped carrot, and potato. Cook for another 5 minutes, allowing the flavors to blend.
4. **Add the broth and spices:** Pour in the vegetable broth, then add cumin, cinnamon, salt, and pepper. Bring the mixture to a boil.
5. **Simmer:** Reduce the heat to low and let the soup simmer for 20-25 minutes, or until the vegetables are tender.
6. **Blend the soup:** Using an immersion blender or regular blender, puree the soup until smooth. If you prefer a chunkier texture, blend only half of the soup.
7. **Add cream (optional):** For a creamier texture, stir in the coconut milk or cream and heat through.
8. **Serve:** Ladle the soup into bowls and garnish with fresh herbs, if desired. Serve warm.

Butternut Squash and Carrot Soup

Ingredients:

- 1 medium butternut squash, peeled, seeded, and cubed
- 3 medium carrots, peeled and chopped
- 1 onion, chopped
- 2 garlic cloves, minced
- 4 cups vegetable or chicken broth
- 1 teaspoon ground ginger
- 1/2 teaspoon ground nutmeg
- Salt and pepper to taste
- 1 tablespoon olive oil
- 1/2 cup coconut milk (optional for creaminess)
- Fresh parsley for garnish (optional)

Instructions:

1. **Sauté vegetables:** In a large pot, heat olive oil over medium heat. Add the chopped onion and garlic, cooking until softened, about 5 minutes.
2. **Cook squash and carrots:** Add the butternut squash and carrots to the pot. Stir to combine, then pour in the broth. Bring to a boil, then reduce the heat and simmer for 20-25 minutes, or until the vegetables are tender.
3. **Blend the soup:** Use an immersion blender or a regular blender to puree the soup until smooth.
4. **Add seasoning:** Stir in ginger, nutmeg, salt, and pepper. If desired, add coconut milk for a creamy texture.
5. **Serve:** Ladle the soup into bowls and garnish with fresh parsley. Serve warm.

Classic Beef Stew

Ingredients:

- 1 lb beef stew meat, cut into 1-inch cubes
- 3 tablespoons flour
- 2 tablespoons olive oil
- 1 onion, chopped
- 2 garlic cloves, minced
- 4 cups beef broth
- 3 carrots, peeled and chopped
- 3 potatoes, peeled and cubed
- 2 celery stalks, chopped
- 1 teaspoon dried thyme
- 1 bay leaf
- Salt and pepper to taste
- 1/2 cup frozen peas (optional)

Instructions:

1. **Brown the beef:** Toss the beef stew meat with flour, salt, and pepper. Heat olive oil in a large pot over medium-high heat. Brown the beef in batches, removing it from the pot as it browns. Set aside.
2. **Cook vegetables:** In the same pot, add onion and garlic, cooking until softened, about 5 minutes.
3. **Simmer stew:** Return the beef to the pot. Add beef broth, carrots, potatoes, celery, thyme, and bay leaf. Bring to a boil, then reduce to a simmer. Cover and cook for 1.5-2 hours, or until the beef is tender.
4. **Finish and serve:** Stir in frozen peas (if using), then cook for an additional 5 minutes. Remove the bay leaf and adjust seasoning with salt and pepper. Serve warm.

Chicken Tortilla Soup

Ingredients:

- 2 tablespoons olive oil
- 1 onion, chopped
- 2 garlic cloves, minced
- 1 bell pepper, chopped
- 1 can (14.5 oz) diced tomatoes
- 4 cups chicken broth
- 2 cups cooked, shredded chicken (rotisserie chicken works well)
- 1 teaspoon ground cumin
- 1 teaspoon chili powder
- 1/2 teaspoon paprika
- Salt and pepper to taste
- 1 cup frozen corn (optional)
- 4-6 corn tortillas, cut into strips
- Fresh lime wedges, cilantro, and avocado for garnish

Instructions:

1. **Cook the vegetables:** Heat olive oil in a large pot over medium heat. Add the onion, garlic, and bell pepper, cooking until softened, about 5 minutes.
2. **Simmer the soup:** Add the diced tomatoes, chicken broth, shredded chicken, cumin, chili powder, paprika, salt, and pepper to the pot. Bring to a boil, then reduce the heat and simmer for 15-20 minutes.
3. **Add corn and tortillas:** Stir in frozen corn (if using) and tortilla strips. Simmer for another 5 minutes, allowing the tortillas to soften and thicken the soup.
4. **Serve:** Ladle the soup into bowls and garnish with fresh lime wedges, cilantro, and avocado slices. Serve hot.

Sweet Potato and Lentil Soup

Ingredients:

- 2 medium sweet potatoes, peeled and diced
- 1 cup dried lentils, rinsed
- 1 onion, chopped
- 2 garlic cloves, minced
- 1 teaspoon ground cumin
- 1 teaspoon turmeric
- 1 teaspoon ground coriander
- 4 cups vegetable broth
- 2 cups water
- Salt and pepper to taste
- 2 tablespoons olive oil
- Fresh parsley for garnish (optional)

Instructions:

1. **Sauté the vegetables:** In a large pot, heat olive oil over medium heat. Add the onion and garlic and cook until softened, about 5 minutes.
2. **Add spices and lentils:** Stir in the cumin, turmeric, coriander, and lentils. Cook for 2-3 minutes to toast the spices.
3. **Add sweet potatoes and broth:** Add the sweet potatoes, vegetable broth, and water. Bring to a boil, then reduce the heat and simmer for 25-30 minutes, or until the lentils and sweet potatoes are tender.
4. **Blend the soup (optional):** For a smoother texture, use an immersion blender to puree the soup, or leave it chunky.
5. **Serve:** Season with salt and pepper, then garnish with fresh parsley. Serve warm.

Spicy Pumpkin Chili

Ingredients:

- 1 can (15 oz) pumpkin puree
- 1 can (15 oz) black beans, drained and rinsed
- 1 can (15 oz) kidney beans, drained and rinsed
- 1 onion, chopped
- 2 garlic cloves, minced
- 1 can (14.5 oz) diced tomatoes
- 1 can (4 oz) diced green chilies
- 2 teaspoons chili powder
- 1 teaspoon ground cumin
- 1/2 teaspoon smoked paprika
- Salt and pepper to taste
- 2 tablespoons olive oil
- 1 cup vegetable broth
- Fresh cilantro for garnish (optional)

Instructions:

1. **Sauté the vegetables:** Heat olive oil in a large pot over medium heat. Add the onion and garlic and cook until softened, about 5 minutes.
2. **Add spices and beans:** Stir in the chili powder, cumin, paprika, black beans, kidney beans, diced tomatoes, and green chilies. Mix well.
3. **Simmer the chili:** Add the pumpkin puree and vegetable broth, then bring the mixture to a boil. Reduce the heat and simmer for 25-30 minutes, stirring occasionally.
4. **Serve:** Season with salt and pepper, then garnish with fresh cilantro. Serve hot.

Creamy Tomato Basil Soup

Ingredients:

- 2 tablespoons olive oil
- 1 onion, chopped
- 2 garlic cloves, minced
- 1 can (28 oz) crushed tomatoes
- 4 cups vegetable broth
- 1 teaspoon dried basil
- 1/2 teaspoon sugar
- 1/2 cup heavy cream
- Salt and pepper to taste
- Fresh basil leaves for garnish (optional)

Instructions:

1. **Sauté the vegetables:** Heat olive oil in a large pot over medium heat. Add the onion and garlic and cook until softened, about 5 minutes.
2. **Add tomatoes and broth:** Stir in the crushed tomatoes, vegetable broth, basil, and sugar. Bring the soup to a simmer and cook for 15-20 minutes.
3. **Blend the soup:** Use an immersion blender or regular blender to puree the soup until smooth.
4. **Add cream and season:** Stir in the heavy cream and season with salt and pepper. Heat through.
5. **Serve:** Garnish with fresh basil leaves and serve warm.

Chicken and Wild Rice Soup

Ingredients:

- 1 lb boneless, skinless chicken breasts
- 1 cup wild rice
- 1 onion, chopped
- 2 carrots, peeled and chopped
- 2 celery stalks, chopped
- 2 garlic cloves, minced
- 4 cups chicken broth
- 1 teaspoon dried thyme
- 1/2 teaspoon dried rosemary
- Salt and pepper to taste
- 1 tablespoon olive oil
- 1/2 cup heavy cream (optional)

Instructions:

1. **Cook the chicken:** In a large pot, heat olive oil over medium heat. Add the chicken breasts and cook for 5-7 minutes per side, until cooked through. Remove from the pot, shred, and set aside.
2. **Sauté the vegetables:** In the same pot, add the onion, carrots, celery, and garlic. Cook for 5 minutes, until softened.
3. **Add rice and broth:** Stir in the wild rice, chicken broth, thyme, rosemary, salt, and pepper. Bring to a boil, then reduce the heat and simmer for 30 minutes, or until the rice is tender.
4. **Finish the soup:** Add the shredded chicken back into the pot. Stir in the heavy cream, if using, and simmer for another 5-10 minutes.
5. **Serve:** Adjust seasoning with salt and pepper, then serve hot.

Autumn Harvest Soup

Ingredients:

- 2 tablespoons olive oil
- 1 onion, chopped
- 2 garlic cloves, minced
- 2 cups butternut squash, peeled and cubed
- 2 carrots, peeled and chopped
- 2 cups apples, peeled and chopped
- 4 cups vegetable broth
- 1 teaspoon dried sage
- 1/2 teaspoon cinnamon
- Salt and pepper to taste
- Fresh thyme for garnish (optional)

Instructions:

1. **Sauté the vegetables:** In a large pot, heat olive oil over medium heat. Add the onion and garlic and cook until softened, about 5 minutes.
2. **Add the vegetables and apples:** Stir in the butternut squash, carrots, and apples. Cook for 5 minutes, stirring occasionally.
3. **Simmer the soup:** Add the vegetable broth, sage, cinnamon, salt, and pepper. Bring to a boil, then reduce to a simmer and cook for 25-30 minutes.
4. **Blend the soup (optional):** Use an immersion blender to puree the soup for a creamy texture, or leave it chunky.
5. **Serve:** Garnish with fresh thyme, if desired, and serve warm.

Butternut Squash Chili

Ingredients:

- 1 medium butternut squash, peeled and cubed
- 1 onion, chopped
- 2 garlic cloves, minced
- 1 can (15 oz) kidney beans, drained and rinsed
- 1 can (15 oz) black beans, drained and rinsed
- 1 can (14.5 oz) diced tomatoes
- 2 teaspoons chili powder
- 1 teaspoon cumin
- Salt and pepper to taste
- 4 cups vegetable broth
- 2 tablespoons olive oil

Instructions:

1. **Sauté the vegetables:** Heat olive oil in a large pot over medium heat. Add the onion and garlic and cook until softened, about 5 minutes.
2. **Add the squash and spices:** Stir in the butternut squash, chili powder, and cumin. Cook for 2-3 minutes to toast the spices.
3. **Add beans and broth:** Add the kidney beans, black beans, diced tomatoes, and vegetable broth. Bring to a boil, then reduce to a simmer and cook for 25-30 minutes, or until the squash is tender.
4. **Serve:** Season with salt and pepper, and serve warm.

Italian Wedding Soup

Ingredients:

- 1/2 lb ground turkey or beef
- 1/2 cup breadcrumbs
- 1 egg
- 1/4 cup grated Parmesan cheese
- 1 onion, chopped
- 2 garlic cloves, minced
- 6 cups chicken broth
- 1 cup small pasta (such as orzo or acini di pepe)
- 2 cups spinach, chopped
- Salt and pepper to taste
- 2 tablespoons olive oil

Instructions:

1. **Make the meatballs:** In a bowl, combine the ground meat, breadcrumbs, egg, Parmesan, salt, and pepper. Form into small meatballs (about 1 inch in diameter).
2. **Sauté the vegetables:** Heat olive oil in a large pot over medium heat. Add the onion and garlic and cook until softened, about 5 minutes.
3. **Cook the meatballs:** Add the chicken broth to the pot and bring to a boil. Gently drop the meatballs into the broth and cook for 10-15 minutes, or until they are cooked through.
4. **Add pasta and spinach:** Stir in the pasta and cook for an additional 8-10 minutes, or until the pasta is tender. Add the spinach and cook for another 2-3 minutes.
5. **Serve:** Season with salt and pepper to taste, and serve warm.

French Onion Soup

Ingredients:

- 4 large onions, thinly sliced
- 2 tablespoons butter
- 1 tablespoon olive oil
- 4 cups beef broth
- 1/2 cup white wine
- 2 teaspoons fresh thyme
- 1 bay leaf
- 4 slices baguette, toasted
- 1 1/2 cups grated Gruyère cheese
- Salt and pepper to taste

Instructions:

1. **Caramelize the onions:** In a large pot, melt the butter and olive oil over medium heat. Add the onions and cook, stirring occasionally, for 30-40 minutes, until the onions are deeply browned and caramelized.
2. **Add the liquids and spices:** Stir in the beef broth, white wine, thyme, and bay leaf. Bring to a boil, then reduce to a simmer and cook for 20 minutes.
3. **Serve:** Ladle the soup into bowls. Top each bowl with a slice of toasted baguette and sprinkle with Gruyère cheese. Place under the broiler for 2-3 minutes, until the cheese is melted and bubbly.
4. **Enjoy:** Season with salt and pepper and serve hot.

Beef and Barley Stew

Ingredients:

- 1 lb beef stew meat, cubed
- 1 cup pearl barley, rinsed
- 2 carrots, peeled and chopped
- 2 celery stalks, chopped
- 1 onion, chopped
- 3 garlic cloves, minced
- 4 cups beef broth
- 1 bay leaf
- 1 teaspoon dried thyme
- Salt and pepper to taste
- 2 tablespoons olive oil

Instructions:

1. **Brown the beef:** In a large pot, heat olive oil over medium-high heat. Add the beef stew meat and brown on all sides, about 5-7 minutes. Remove the beef and set aside.
2. **Sauté the vegetables:** In the same pot, add the onion, carrots, celery, and garlic. Cook for 5 minutes, until softened.
3. **Simmer the stew:** Add the beef back into the pot along with the barley, beef broth, bay leaf, thyme, salt, and pepper. Bring to a boil, then reduce the heat and simmer for 1-1.5 hours, or until the barley and beef are tender.
4. **Serve:** Adjust seasoning and serve hot.

Vegetable and Quinoa Soup

Ingredients:

- 1 cup quinoa, rinsed
- 2 carrots, peeled and chopped
- 2 celery stalks, chopped
- 1 onion, chopped
- 1 zucchini, chopped
- 1 can (14.5 oz) diced tomatoes
- 4 cups vegetable broth
- 2 teaspoons dried oregano
- 1 teaspoon ground cumin
- Salt and pepper to taste
- 2 tablespoons olive oil

Instructions:

1. **Sauté the vegetables:** In a large pot, heat olive oil over medium heat. Add the onion, carrots, and celery and cook for 5-7 minutes until softened.
2. **Add remaining ingredients:** Stir in the zucchini, quinoa, diced tomatoes, vegetable broth, oregano, cumin, salt, and pepper. Bring to a boil, then reduce the heat and simmer for 20-25 minutes, or until the quinoa and vegetables are tender.
3. **Serve:** Adjust seasoning and serve warm.

Sausage and White Bean Stew

Ingredients:

- 1 lb Italian sausage, casings removed
- 1 can (15 oz) white beans, drained and rinsed
- 1 onion, chopped
- 2 garlic cloves, minced
- 2 cups chicken broth
- 2 cups spinach, chopped
- 1 teaspoon dried oregano
- Salt and pepper to taste
- 2 tablespoons olive oil

Instructions:

1. **Brown the sausage:** In a large pot, heat olive oil over medium heat. Add the sausage and cook, breaking it up with a spoon, until browned.
2. **Sauté the vegetables:** Add the onion and garlic to the pot and cook until softened, about 5 minutes.
3. **Simmer the stew:** Stir in the white beans, chicken broth, spinach, oregano, salt, and pepper. Bring to a boil, then reduce to a simmer and cook for 15-20 minutes.
4. **Serve:** Adjust seasoning and serve hot.

Chicken and Corn Chowder

Ingredients:

- 2 cups cooked chicken, shredded
- 2 cups frozen corn kernels
- 1 onion, chopped
- 2 garlic cloves, minced
- 3 potatoes, peeled and diced
- 4 cups chicken broth
- 1 cup half-and-half
- 1 teaspoon dried thyme
- Salt and pepper to taste
- 2 tablespoons butter

Instructions:

1. **Sauté the vegetables:** In a large pot, melt butter over medium heat. Add the onion and garlic and cook until softened, about 5 minutes.
2. **Add potatoes and broth:** Stir in the potatoes, chicken broth, thyme, salt, and pepper. Bring to a boil, then reduce the heat and simmer for 15-20 minutes, or until the potatoes are tender.
3. **Add chicken and corn:** Stir in the cooked chicken and corn. Simmer for 10 minutes, then stir in the half-and-half.
4. **Serve:** Adjust seasoning and serve hot.

Apple and Bacon Soup

Ingredients:

- 6 slices bacon, chopped
- 1 onion, chopped
- 2 apples, peeled, cored, and chopped
- 4 cups chicken broth
- 1/2 teaspoon ground cinnamon
- Salt and pepper to taste
- 1/2 cup heavy cream (optional)

Instructions:

1. **Cook the bacon:** In a large pot, cook the bacon over medium heat until crispy. Remove and set aside, leaving some bacon drippings in the pot.
2. **Sauté the onion and apples:** Add the onion to the pot and cook for 5 minutes. Stir in the apples, cinnamon, salt, and pepper, and cook for another 5 minutes.
3. **Simmer the soup:** Add the chicken broth and bring to a boil. Reduce the heat and simmer for 15-20 minutes until the apples are soft.
4. **Blend the soup:** Use an immersion blender or regular blender to puree the soup until smooth. Stir in the heavy cream if desired.
5. **Serve:** Garnish with crumbled bacon and serve hot.

Potato Leek Soup

Ingredients:

- 4 large potatoes, peeled and diced
- 2 leeks, cleaned and sliced
- 1 onion, chopped
- 2 garlic cloves, minced
- 4 cups vegetable broth
- 1 cup heavy cream
- Salt and pepper to taste
- 2 tablespoons butter

Instructions:

1. **Sauté the vegetables:** In a large pot, melt butter over medium heat. Add the leeks, onion, and garlic and cook for 5 minutes until softened.
2. **Add potatoes and broth:** Stir in the potatoes, vegetable broth, salt, and pepper. Bring to a boil, then reduce the heat and simmer for 20 minutes, or until the potatoes are tender.
3. **Blend the soup:** Use an immersion blender or regular blender to puree the soup until smooth.
4. **Finish the soup:** Stir in the heavy cream and cook for an additional 5 minutes.
5. **Serve:** Adjust seasoning and serve warm.

Split Pea Soup with Ham

Ingredients:

- 1 lb dried split peas, rinsed
- 2 cups cooked ham, diced
- 1 onion, chopped
- 2 garlic cloves, minced
- 4 cups chicken broth
- 2 carrots, peeled and chopped
- 2 celery stalks, chopped
- 1 bay leaf
- Salt and pepper to taste
- 2 tablespoons olive oil

Instructions:

1. **Sauté the vegetables:** In a large pot, heat olive oil over medium heat. Add the onion, garlic, carrots, and celery and cook until softened, about 5 minutes.
2. **Simmer the soup:** Add the split peas, ham, chicken broth, bay leaf, salt, and pepper. Bring to a boil, then reduce the heat and simmer for 45-60 minutes, or until the peas are tender.
3. **Serve:** Remove the bay leaf, adjust seasoning, and serve hot.

Harvest Chicken Stew

Ingredients:

- 2 cups cooked chicken, shredded
- 2 sweet potatoes, peeled and cubed
- 2 carrots, peeled and chopped
- 1 onion, chopped
- 3 garlic cloves, minced
- 4 cups chicken broth
- 2 teaspoons dried thyme
- Salt and pepper to taste
- 2 tablespoons olive oil

Instructions:

1. **Sauté the vegetables:** In a large pot, heat olive oil over medium heat. Add the onion and garlic and cook until softened, about 5 minutes.
2. **Add sweet potatoes and carrots:** Stir in the sweet potatoes and carrots, and cook for 5 minutes.
3. **Simmer the stew:** Add the chicken, chicken broth, thyme, salt, and pepper. Bring to a boil, then reduce the heat and simmer for 30 minutes or until the vegetables are tender.
4. **Serve:** Adjust seasoning and serve hot.

Sweet Potato and Black Bean Chili

Ingredients:

- 2 sweet potatoes, peeled and cubed
- 1 can (15 oz) black beans, drained and rinsed
- 1 onion, chopped
- 2 garlic cloves, minced
- 1 can (14.5 oz) diced tomatoes
- 1 can (4 oz) diced green chilies
- 2 teaspoons chili powder
- 1 teaspoon cumin
- Salt and pepper to taste
- 4 cups vegetable broth
- 2 tablespoons olive oil

Instructions:

1. **Sauté the vegetables:** In a large pot, heat olive oil over medium heat. Add the onion and garlic and cook until softened, about 5 minutes.
2. **Add sweet potatoes and spices:** Stir in the sweet potatoes, chili powder, and cumin, and cook for 5 minutes to toast the spices.
3. **Simmer the chili:** Add the black beans, diced tomatoes, green chilies, vegetable broth, salt, and pepper. Bring to a boil, then reduce the heat and simmer for 25-30 minutes, until the sweet potatoes are tender.
4. **Serve:** Adjust seasoning and serve hot.

Cabbage Roll Soup

Ingredients:

- 1 lb ground beef or turkey
- 1 onion, chopped
- 1 garlic clove, minced
- 1 can (15 oz) diced tomatoes
- 1 can (15 oz) tomato sauce
- 4 cups beef broth
- 1/2 head cabbage, chopped
- 1/2 cup rice (uncooked)
- 1 teaspoon dried thyme
- Salt and pepper to taste
- 2 tablespoons olive oil

Instructions:

1. **Cook the meat:** In a large pot, heat olive oil over medium heat. Add the ground beef or turkey and cook, breaking it up with a spoon until browned.
2. **Sauté the vegetables:** Add the onion and garlic to the pot and cook until softened, about 5 minutes.
3. **Simmer the soup:** Stir in the diced tomatoes, tomato sauce, beef broth, cabbage, rice, thyme, salt, and pepper. Bring to a boil, then reduce to a simmer and cook for 30 minutes, or until the rice and cabbage are tender.
4. **Serve:** Adjust seasoning and serve hot.

Tuscan Bean and Kale Soup

Ingredients:

- 1 can (15 oz) white beans, drained and rinsed
- 2 cups kale, chopped
- 1 onion, chopped
- 2 garlic cloves, minced
- 2 carrots, peeled and chopped
- 1 zucchini, chopped
- 4 cups vegetable broth
- 1 teaspoon dried oregano
- 1 teaspoon dried rosemary
- Salt and pepper to taste
- 2 tablespoons olive oil

Instructions:

1. **Sauté the vegetables:** In a large pot, heat olive oil over medium heat. Add the onion, carrots, zucchini, and garlic and cook until softened, about 5 minutes.
2. **Add the beans and broth:** Stir in the white beans, vegetable broth, oregano, rosemary, salt, and pepper. Bring to a boil, then reduce the heat and simmer for 15-20 minutes.
3. **Add the kale:** Stir in the kale and cook for another 5 minutes, until wilted.
4. **Serve:** Adjust seasoning and serve hot.

Mushroom and Barley Soup

Ingredients:

- 2 cups mushrooms, sliced
- 1 cup barley, rinsed
- 1 onion, chopped
- 2 garlic cloves, minced
- 4 cups vegetable broth
- 1 teaspoon dried thyme
- Salt and pepper to taste
- 2 tablespoons olive oil

Instructions:

1. **Sauté the mushrooms:** In a large pot, heat olive oil over medium heat. Add the mushrooms and cook until softened and browned, about 5 minutes.
2. **Sauté the onions and garlic:** Add the onion and garlic to the pot and cook for 5 minutes, until softened.
3. **Simmer the soup:** Stir in the barley, vegetable broth, thyme, salt, and pepper. Bring to a boil, then reduce the heat and simmer for 30-40 minutes, or until the barley is tender.
4. **Serve:** Adjust seasoning and serve hot.

Beef and Sweet Potato Stew

Ingredients:

- 1 lb beef stew meat, cubed
- 2 sweet potatoes, peeled and cubed
- 2 carrots, peeled and chopped
- 1 onion, chopped
- 3 garlic cloves, minced
- 4 cups beef broth
- 1 teaspoon dried rosemary
- Salt and pepper to taste
- 2 tablespoons olive oil

Instructions:

1. **Brown the beef:** In a large pot, heat olive oil over medium-high heat. Add the beef stew meat and brown on all sides, about 5-7 minutes. Remove the beef and set aside.
2. **Sauté the vegetables:** In the same pot, add the onion, garlic, carrots, and sweet potatoes. Cook for 5 minutes.
3. **Simmer the stew:** Add the beef back into the pot along with the beef broth, rosemary, salt, and pepper. Bring to a boil, then reduce the heat and simmer for 1 hour, or until the beef and sweet potatoes are tender.
4. **Serve:** Adjust seasoning and serve hot.

Curried Butternut Squash Soup

Ingredients:

- 1 butternut squash, peeled, seeded, and cubed
- 1 onion, chopped
- 2 garlic cloves, minced
- 1 teaspoon ground curry powder
- 4 cups vegetable broth
- 1 cup coconut milk
- Salt and pepper to taste
- 2 tablespoons olive oil

Instructions:

1. **Roast the squash:** Preheat the oven to 400°F (200°C). Toss the butternut squash cubes with 1 tablespoon olive oil, salt, and pepper. Spread on a baking sheet and roast for 25-30 minutes, until tender.
2. **Sauté the vegetables:** In a large pot, heat the remaining olive oil over medium heat. Add the onion and garlic and cook for 5 minutes until softened. Stir in the curry powder and cook for 1 minute.
3. **Simmer the soup:** Add the roasted squash, vegetable broth, and coconut milk to the pot. Bring to a boil, then reduce to a simmer and cook for 10 minutes.
4. **Blend the soup:** Use an immersion blender or regular blender to puree the soup until smooth.
5. **Serve:** Adjust seasoning and serve hot.

Bacon and Potato Soup

Ingredients:

- 6 slices bacon, chopped
- 4 potatoes, peeled and diced
- 1 onion, chopped
- 3 garlic cloves, minced
- 4 cups chicken broth
- 1 cup heavy cream
- Salt and pepper to taste
- 2 tablespoons olive oil

Instructions:

1. **Cook the bacon:** In a large pot, cook the bacon over medium heat until crispy. Remove and set aside, leaving some bacon drippings in the pot.
2. **Sauté the vegetables:** Add the onion and garlic to the pot and cook for 5 minutes. Stir in the potatoes, chicken broth, salt, and pepper. Bring to a boil, then reduce the heat and simmer for 15-20 minutes, or until the potatoes are tender.
3. **Finish the soup:** Stir in the heavy cream and cook for an additional 5 minutes.
4. **Serve:** Garnish with the cooked bacon and serve hot.

Carrot Ginger Soup

Ingredients:

- 6 carrots, peeled and chopped
- 1 onion, chopped
- 2 garlic cloves, minced
- 1-inch piece of fresh ginger, grated
- 4 cups vegetable broth
- Salt and pepper to taste
- 2 tablespoons olive oil

Instructions:

1. **Sauté the vegetables:** In a large pot, heat olive oil over medium heat. Add the onion and garlic and cook until softened, about 5 minutes. Stir in the ginger and cook for 1 minute.
2. **Simmer the soup:** Add the carrots and vegetable broth to the pot. Bring to a boil, then reduce the heat and simmer for 20-25 minutes, until the carrots are tender.
3. **Blend the soup:** Use an immersion blender or regular blender to puree the soup until smooth.
4. **Serve:** Adjust seasoning and serve hot.

Zucchini and Tomato Stew

Ingredients:

- 4 zucchinis, chopped
- 2 tomatoes, chopped
- 1 onion, chopped
- 2 garlic cloves, minced
- 4 cups vegetable broth
- 1 teaspoon dried oregano
- Salt and pepper to taste
- 2 tablespoons olive oil

Instructions:

1. **Sauté the vegetables:** In a large pot, heat olive oil over medium heat. Add the onion and garlic and cook until softened, about 5 minutes.
2. **Add zucchini and tomatoes:** Stir in the zucchini and tomatoes and cook for 5 minutes.
3. **Simmer the stew:** Add the vegetable broth, oregano, salt, and pepper. Bring to a boil, then reduce the heat and simmer for 15-20 minutes, until the zucchini is tender.
4. **Serve:** Adjust seasoning and serve hot.

Spaghetti Squash and Sausage Soup

Ingredients:

- 1 spaghetti squash, roasted and shredded
- 1 lb Italian sausage, casings removed
- 1 onion, chopped
- 2 garlic cloves, minced
- 4 cups chicken broth
- 1 teaspoon dried thyme
- Salt and pepper to taste
- 2 tablespoons olive oil

Instructions:

1. **Prepare the spaghetti squash:** Preheat the oven to 400°F (200°C). Cut the spaghetti squash in half and remove the seeds. Drizzle with olive oil, season with salt and pepper, and roast cut-side down for 30-40 minutes until tender. Shred the flesh with a fork to create "spaghetti."
2. **Cook the sausage:** In a large pot, heat olive oil over medium heat. Add the sausage and cook, breaking it up with a spoon, until browned.
3. **Sauté the vegetables:** Add the onion and garlic to the pot and cook until softened, about 5 minutes.
4. **Simmer the soup:** Add the chicken broth, thyme, shredded spaghetti squash, salt, and pepper. Bring to a boil, then reduce to a simmer for 10-15 minutes.
5. **Serve:** Adjust seasoning and serve hot.

Harvest Pumpkin Chili

Ingredients:

- 1 can (15 oz) pumpkin puree
- 1 lb ground turkey or beef
- 1 onion, chopped
- 1 bell pepper, chopped
- 2 garlic cloves, minced
- 1 can (15 oz) kidney beans, drained and rinsed
- 1 can (15 oz) diced tomatoes
- 1 tablespoon chili powder
- 1 teaspoon cumin
- Salt and pepper to taste
- 2 tablespoons olive oil

Instructions:

1. **Cook the meat:** In a large pot, heat olive oil over medium heat. Add the ground turkey or beef and cook until browned, breaking it up with a spoon.
2. **Sauté the vegetables:** Add the onion, bell pepper, and garlic and cook until softened, about 5 minutes.
3. **Simmer the chili:** Stir in the pumpkin puree, kidney beans, diced tomatoes, chili powder, cumin, salt, and pepper. Bring to a boil, then reduce to a simmer and cook for 25-30 minutes.
4. **Serve:** Adjust seasoning and serve hot.

Corn and Potato Chowder

Ingredients:

- 4 cups corn kernels (fresh or frozen)
- 4 potatoes, peeled and diced
- 1 onion, chopped
- 2 garlic cloves, minced
- 4 cups vegetable or chicken broth
- 1 cup heavy cream
- Salt and pepper to taste
- 2 tablespoons butter

Instructions:

1. **Sauté the vegetables:** In a large pot, melt the butter over medium heat. Add the onion and garlic and cook until softened, about 5 minutes.
2. **Simmer the chowder:** Add the corn, potatoes, broth, salt, and pepper to the pot. Bring to a boil, then reduce to a simmer and cook for 20-25 minutes, until the potatoes are tender.
3. **Finish the chowder:** Stir in the heavy cream and cook for an additional 5 minutes.
4. **Serve:** Adjust seasoning and serve hot.

Chicken Gnocchi Soup

Ingredients:

- 2 cups cooked chicken, shredded
- 1 package gnocchi
- 1 onion, chopped
- 2 garlic cloves, minced
- 4 cups chicken broth
- 2 cups spinach, chopped
- 1 cup heavy cream
- Salt and pepper to taste
- 2 tablespoons olive oil

Instructions:

1. **Sauté the vegetables:** In a large pot, heat olive oil over medium heat. Add the onion and garlic and cook until softened, about 5 minutes.
2. **Simmer the soup:** Add the chicken, gnocchi, chicken broth, salt, and pepper. Bring to a boil, then reduce to a simmer and cook for 10 minutes.
3. **Finish the soup:** Stir in the spinach and heavy cream and cook for an additional 5 minutes.
4. **Serve:** Adjust seasoning and serve hot.

Tomato and Roasted Red Pepper Soup

Ingredients:

- 2 cups roasted red peppers, chopped
- 4 tomatoes, chopped
- 1 onion, chopped
- 2 garlic cloves, minced
- 4 cups vegetable or chicken broth
- 1 teaspoon dried basil
- Salt and pepper to taste
- 2 tablespoons olive oil

Instructions:

1. **Sauté the vegetables:** In a large pot, heat olive oil over medium heat. Add the onion and garlic and cook until softened, about 5 minutes.
2. **Simmer the soup:** Stir in the roasted red peppers, tomatoes, broth, basil, salt, and pepper. Bring to a boil, then reduce to a simmer and cook for 20-25 minutes.
3. **Blend the soup:** Use an immersion blender or regular blender to puree the soup until smooth.
4. **Serve:** Adjust seasoning and serve hot.

White Bean and Sausage Soup

Ingredients:

- 1 lb Italian sausage, casings removed
- 2 cans (15 oz) white beans, drained and rinsed
- 1 onion, chopped
- 2 garlic cloves, minced
- 4 cups chicken broth
- 1 teaspoon dried thyme
- Salt and pepper to taste
- 2 tablespoons olive oil

Instructions:

1. **Cook the sausage:** In a large pot, heat olive oil over medium heat. Add the sausage and cook, breaking it up with a spoon, until browned.
2. **Sauté the vegetables:** Add the onion and garlic and cook until softened, about 5 minutes.
3. **Simmer the soup:** Stir in the white beans, chicken broth, thyme, salt, and pepper. Bring to a boil, then reduce to a simmer and cook for 15-20 minutes.
4. **Serve:** Adjust seasoning and serve hot.

Lamb and Vegetable Stew

Ingredients:

- 1 lb lamb stew meat, cubed
- 2 carrots, peeled and chopped
- 2 potatoes, peeled and diced
- 1 onion, chopped
- 2 garlic cloves, minced
- 4 cups beef broth
- 1 teaspoon dried rosemary
- Salt and pepper to taste
- 2 tablespoons olive oil

Instructions:

1. **Brown the lamb:** In a large pot, heat olive oil over medium-high heat. Add the lamb stew meat and brown on all sides, about 5-7 minutes. Remove the lamb and set aside.
2. **Sauté the vegetables:** In the same pot, add the onion, garlic, carrots, and potatoes. Cook for 5 minutes.
3. **Simmer the stew:** Add the lamb back into the pot along with the beef broth, rosemary, salt, and pepper. Bring to a boil, then reduce the heat and simmer for 1 hour, or until the lamb is tender.
4. **Serve:** Adjust seasoning and serve hot.

Pork and Apple Stew

Ingredients:

- 1 lb pork stew meat, cubed
- 2 apples, peeled and chopped
- 1 onion, chopped
- 2 garlic cloves, minced
- 4 cups chicken broth
- 1 teaspoon dried sage
- Salt and pepper to taste
- 2 tablespoons olive oil

Instructions:

1. **Brown the pork:** In a large pot, heat olive oil over medium-high heat. Add the pork stew meat and brown on all sides, about 5-7 minutes. Remove the pork and set aside.
2. **Sauté the vegetables:** In the same pot, add the onion, garlic, and apples. Cook for 5 minutes.
3. **Simmer the stew:** Add the pork back into the pot along with the chicken broth, sage, salt, and pepper. Bring to a boil, then reduce the heat and simmer for 45 minutes, or until the pork is tender.
4. **Serve:** Adjust seasoning and serve hot.

Turkey and Sweet Potato Soup

Ingredients:

- 1 lb ground turkey
- 2 sweet potatoes, peeled and diced
- 1 onion, chopped
- 2 garlic cloves, minced
- 4 cups chicken broth
- 1 teaspoon dried thyme
- Salt and pepper to taste
- 2 tablespoons olive oil

Instructions:

1. **Cook the turkey:** In a large pot, heat olive oil over medium heat. Add the ground turkey and cook, breaking it up with a spoon, until browned.
2. **Sauté the vegetables:** Add the onion and garlic to the pot and cook for 5 minutes.
3. **Simmer the soup:** Stir in the sweet potatoes, chicken broth, thyme, salt, and pepper. Bring to a boil, then reduce to a simmer and cook for 25-30 minutes, until the sweet potatoes are tender.
4. **Serve:** Adjust seasoning and serve hot.

Beef and Mushroom Stew

Ingredients:

- 1 lb beef stew meat, cubed
- 2 cups mushrooms, sliced
- 1 onion, chopped
- 2 garlic cloves, minced
- 4 cups beef broth
- 2 carrots, peeled and chopped
- 2 potatoes, peeled and diced
- 1 teaspoon dried thyme
- Salt and pepper to taste
- 2 tablespoons olive oil

Instructions:

1. **Brown the beef:** In a large pot, heat olive oil over medium-high heat. Add the beef stew meat and brown on all sides, about 5-7 minutes. Remove the beef and set aside.
2. **Sauté the vegetables:** In the same pot, add the onion, garlic, and mushrooms. Cook for 5 minutes, until softened.
3. **Simmer the stew:** Add the beef back into the pot along with the beef broth, carrots, potatoes, thyme, salt, and pepper. Bring to a boil, then reduce to a simmer and cook for 1-1.5 hours, until the beef is tender.
4. **Serve:** Adjust seasoning and serve hot.

Creamy Broccoli Cheddar Soup

Ingredients:

- 4 cups broccoli florets
- 1 onion, chopped
- 2 garlic cloves, minced
- 4 cups vegetable broth
- 2 cups milk
- 1.5 cups shredded cheddar cheese
- 2 tablespoons butter
- 2 tablespoons flour
- Salt and pepper to taste

Instructions:

1. **Cook the vegetables:** In a large pot, melt butter over medium heat. Add the onion and garlic, cooking until softened, about 5 minutes.
2. **Make the roux:** Stir in the flour and cook for 1-2 minutes. Gradually add the vegetable broth, stirring constantly to avoid lumps.
3. **Simmer the soup:** Add the broccoli florets and cook for 10-15 minutes until tender.
4. **Blend the soup:** Use an immersion blender to puree the soup, or blend in batches until smooth.
5. **Finish the soup:** Stir in the milk and shredded cheddar cheese until the cheese melts and the soup is creamy. Adjust seasoning with salt and pepper.
6. **Serve:** Serve hot with extra cheddar cheese if desired.

Chicken and Dumplings

Ingredients:

- 2 cups cooked chicken, shredded
- 4 cups chicken broth
- 1 onion, chopped
- 2 garlic cloves, minced
- 2 carrots, peeled and chopped
- 1 cup frozen peas
- 1 teaspoon dried thyme
- 1 cup flour
- 2 teaspoons baking powder
- 1/2 teaspoon salt
- 1/2 cup milk
- 1/4 cup butter

Instructions:

1. **Prepare the base:** In a large pot, heat butter over medium heat. Add the onion, garlic, and carrots and cook for 5 minutes until softened.
2. **Simmer the broth:** Add the chicken broth, thyme, and shredded chicken. Bring to a simmer and cook for 15 minutes.
3. **Make the dumplings:** In a bowl, combine the flour, baking powder, salt, and milk to make a dough. Drop spoonfuls of the dough into the simmering broth.
4. **Cook the dumplings:** Cover the pot and cook for 15-20 minutes, or until the dumplings are cooked through.
5. **Finish the soup:** Stir in the peas and cook for another 2-3 minutes. Adjust seasoning with salt and pepper.
6. **Serve:** Serve hot.

Pork Posole

Ingredients:

- 1 lb pork shoulder, cubed
- 1 can (15 oz) hominy, drained and rinsed
- 1 onion, chopped
- 2 garlic cloves, minced
- 4 cups chicken broth
- 1 teaspoon ground cumin
- 1 teaspoon chili powder
- 1/2 teaspoon dried oregano
- Salt and pepper to taste
- 2 tablespoons olive oil
- 1 lime, cut into wedges (for serving)
- Fresh cilantro (optional, for garnish)

Instructions:

1. **Brown the pork:** In a large pot, heat olive oil over medium-high heat. Add the pork cubes and brown on all sides, about 5-7 minutes. Remove the pork and set aside.
2. **Sauté the vegetables:** Add the onion and garlic to the pot and cook until softened, about 5 minutes.
3. **Simmer the posole:** Add the pork back into the pot along with the hominy, chicken broth, cumin, chili powder, oregano, salt, and pepper. Bring to a boil, then reduce to a simmer and cook for 1-1.5 hours, until the pork is tender.
4. **Serve:** Serve hot with lime wedges and cilantro, if desired.

Spicy Black Bean Soup

Ingredients:

- 2 cans (15 oz) black beans, drained and rinsed
- 1 onion, chopped
- 2 garlic cloves, minced
- 1 jalapeño, seeded and chopped
- 4 cups vegetable broth
- 1 teaspoon ground cumin
- 1 teaspoon chili powder
- 1 teaspoon smoked paprika
- Salt and pepper to taste
- 2 tablespoons olive oil
- Fresh cilantro (optional, for garnish)

Instructions:

1. **Sauté the vegetables:** In a large pot, heat olive oil over medium heat. Add the onion, garlic, and jalapeño and cook until softened, about 5 minutes.
2. **Simmer the soup:** Add the black beans, vegetable broth, cumin, chili powder, smoked paprika, salt, and pepper. Bring to a boil, then reduce to a simmer and cook for 20-25 minutes.
3. **Blend the soup:** Use an immersion blender to puree the soup to your desired consistency (smooth or chunky).
4. **Serve:** Serve hot, garnished with fresh cilantro if desired.

Ham and Bean Soup

Ingredients:

- 2 cups cooked ham, cubed
- 2 cans (15 oz) white beans, drained and rinsed
- 1 onion, chopped
- 2 garlic cloves, minced
- 4 cups chicken broth
- 2 carrots, peeled and chopped
- 1 teaspoon dried thyme
- Salt and pepper to taste
- 2 tablespoons olive oil

Instructions:

1. **Sauté the vegetables:** In a large pot, heat olive oil over medium heat. Add the onion, garlic, and carrots and cook until softened, about 5 minutes.
2. **Simmer the soup:** Add the ham, white beans, chicken broth, thyme, salt, and pepper. Bring to a boil, then reduce to a simmer and cook for 20-25 minutes.
3. **Serve:** Adjust seasoning and serve hot.

Chicken and Kale Stew

Ingredients:

- 1 lb chicken breast or thighs, cubed
- 4 cups chicken broth
- 2 cups kale, chopped
- 2 carrots, peeled and chopped
- 1 onion, chopped
- 2 garlic cloves, minced
- 1 teaspoon dried thyme
- 1 teaspoon dried rosemary
- Salt and pepper to taste
- 2 tablespoons olive oil
- 1/2 cup heavy cream (optional)

Instructions:

1. **Sauté the chicken:** Heat olive oil in a large pot over medium-high heat. Add the chicken and cook until browned, about 5-7 minutes. Remove and set aside.
2. **Sauté the vegetables:** In the same pot, add the onion, garlic, and carrots. Cook for 5 minutes until softened.
3. **Simmer the stew:** Add the chicken back into the pot, along with the chicken broth, kale, thyme, rosemary, salt, and pepper. Bring to a boil, then reduce to a simmer and cook for 20-25 minutes, until the vegetables are tender.
4. **Finish the stew:** Stir in the heavy cream, if using, and cook for another 2-3 minutes.
5. **Serve:** Adjust seasoning as needed and serve hot.

Wild Rice and Mushroom Soup

Ingredients:

- 1 cup wild rice, rinsed
- 2 cups mushrooms, sliced
- 1 onion, chopped
- 2 garlic cloves, minced
- 4 cups vegetable broth
- 2 cups water
- 1 teaspoon dried thyme
- 1/2 teaspoon ground black pepper
- Salt to taste
- 2 tablespoons butter
- 1/2 cup heavy cream (optional)

Instructions:

1. **Cook the rice:** In a pot, bring 4 cups of water to a boil, then add the wild rice. Reduce the heat and simmer for 40-45 minutes, until the rice is tender. Drain any excess water.
2. **Sauté the vegetables:** While the rice cooks, melt butter in a large pot over medium heat. Add the onion, garlic, and mushrooms. Cook for 7-10 minutes until the mushrooms are softened.
3. **Simmer the soup:** Add the vegetable broth, cooked wild rice, thyme, black pepper, and salt. Bring to a boil, then reduce to a simmer for 15 minutes.
4. **Finish the soup:** Stir in the heavy cream (if using) and cook for another 2-3 minutes.
5. **Serve:** Adjust seasoning to taste and serve hot.

Pumpkin and Sage Soup

Ingredients:

- 4 cups pumpkin puree
- 1 onion, chopped
- 2 garlic cloves, minced
- 4 cups vegetable broth
- 1 teaspoon dried sage
- 1/2 teaspoon ground nutmeg
- 1/2 teaspoon ground cinnamon
- Salt and pepper to taste
- 2 tablespoons olive oil
- 1/2 cup heavy cream (optional)

Instructions:

1. **Sauté the vegetables:** Heat olive oil in a large pot over medium heat. Add the onion and garlic, cooking until softened, about 5 minutes.
2. **Simmer the soup:** Add the pumpkin puree, vegetable broth, sage, nutmeg, cinnamon, salt, and pepper. Bring to a boil, then reduce to a simmer and cook for 15 minutes.
3. **Blend the soup:** Use an immersion blender to puree the soup until smooth (or blend in batches).
4. **Finish the soup:** Stir in the heavy cream, if using, and cook for an additional 2-3 minutes.
5. **Serve:** Adjust seasoning to taste and serve hot.

Shrimp and Corn Chowder

Ingredients:

- 1 lb shrimp, peeled and deveined
- 2 cups corn kernels (fresh or frozen)
- 4 cups chicken or vegetable broth
- 1 onion, chopped
- 2 garlic cloves, minced
- 2 potatoes, peeled and diced
- 1 teaspoon dried thyme
- 1/2 teaspoon smoked paprika
- 2 cups half-and-half
- Salt and pepper to taste
- 2 tablespoons butter

Instructions:

1. **Sauté the shrimp:** In a large pot, melt butter over medium heat. Add the shrimp and cook until pink, about 3-4 minutes. Remove and set aside.
2. **Sauté the vegetables:** In the same pot, add the onion, garlic, and potatoes. Cook for 5-7 minutes until softened.
3. **Simmer the chowder:** Add the broth, corn, thyme, paprika, salt, and pepper. Bring to a boil, then reduce to a simmer and cook for 15 minutes, until the potatoes are tender.
4. **Finish the chowder:** Stir in the half-and-half and return the shrimp to the pot. Cook for another 2-3 minutes.
5. **Serve:** Adjust seasoning to taste and serve hot.

Roasted Vegetable Soup

Ingredients:

- 2 cups carrots, peeled and chopped
- 2 cups parsnips, peeled and chopped
- 1 onion, chopped
- 2 garlic cloves, minced
- 4 cups vegetable broth
- 1 teaspoon dried thyme
- Salt and pepper to taste
- 2 tablespoons olive oil
- 1/2 cup heavy cream (optional)

Instructions:

1. **Roast the vegetables:** Preheat your oven to 400°F (200°C). Toss the carrots, parsnips, and onion with olive oil, salt, and pepper. Spread on a baking sheet and roast for 25-30 minutes, until tender and lightly browned.
2. **Sauté the garlic:** In a large pot, heat a little olive oil over medium heat. Add the garlic and sauté for 1-2 minutes.
3. **Simmer the soup:** Add the roasted vegetables and vegetable broth to the pot. Stir in thyme, salt, and pepper. Bring to a boil, then reduce to a simmer for 10 minutes.
4. **Blend the soup:** Use an immersion blender or regular blender to puree the soup until smooth.
5. **Finish the soup:** Stir in heavy cream (if using) and cook for another 2-3 minutes.
6. **Serve:** Adjust seasoning to taste and serve hot.

Brussels Sprouts and Bacon Soup

Ingredients:

- 1 lb Brussels sprouts, trimmed and halved
- 4 slices bacon, chopped
- 1 onion, chopped
- 2 garlic cloves, minced
- 4 cups chicken broth
- 1 teaspoon dried thyme
- Salt and pepper to taste
- 2 tablespoons olive oil
- 1/2 cup heavy cream (optional)

Instructions:

1. **Cook the bacon:** In a large pot, cook the bacon over medium heat until crispy, about 5-7 minutes. Remove and set aside, leaving the bacon drippings in the pot.
2. **Sauté the vegetables:** Add the Brussels sprouts, onion, and garlic to the pot. Cook for 5-7 minutes, stirring occasionally, until the Brussels sprouts are lightly browned.
3. **Simmer the soup:** Add the chicken broth, thyme, salt, and pepper. Bring to a boil, then reduce to a simmer and cook for 15-20 minutes, until the Brussels sprouts are tender.
4. **Finish the soup:** Stir in the heavy cream (if using) and cook for another 2-3 minutes.
5. **Serve:** Top with crispy bacon and serve hot.